FAI

Faith
for all
Life's Storms

BENSON IDAHOSA

KINGSWAY PUBLICATIONS

EASTBOURNE

Printed in Great Britain for
KINGSWAY PUBLICATIONS LTD
Lottbridge Drove, Eastbourne, E. Sussex BN23 6NT by
Clays Ltd, St Ives plc
Typeset by J&L Composition Ltd, Filey, North Yorkshire.

Contents

1

The Storms of Life

All through this book I want to share with you timeless truths and principles about how you can overcome the storms of life. It is my very strong belief that if you learn the *why*, you will from all standpoints have a better chance to find the *how* to diffuse your storms. Your storms must not overcome you; you must overcome them! I'm going to reveal to you secrets about how to deal with struggles and storms. I am not an imitator. I am a pathmaker and *possibilitarian*.

Storms of life are real, not imaginary stories from children's fairy tales.

For nearly three decades and in some one hundred nations of the world, I have met people from different educational, racial, cultural, and religious backgrounds. One thing I discovered early in the ministry, and in my Christian walk, is that the devil operates the same way around the world.

In the same vein, I also found out that men and

women in every society face struggles and storms of life. No one is exempt.

The most interesting aspect to me is the noble fact that everyone wants to know how to overcome the storms of life.

If there is any way man could avoid the struggles and storms of life, he would no doubt choose that easy path. We all know that there is no such thing as a 'storm-free' life. Therefore, agreeing that there is not a storm-free life on earth, then the only viable alternative open to you under the circumstances is to learn how to take control of the storm.

You see, my friend, the Christian religion is so bogged down in endless theological traditions and archaic ideas that society has almost relegated God and miracles to something of a legend or near superstition. However, every simple mind can read from the New Testament that Christianity and miracles are synonymous.

I have witnessed on a daily basis abundant proof that God is real, that Jesus Christ is alive, that his mighty miracle-working power is unchanged today.

Do you really know what your problem is as a born-again Christian?

Is it to hear God say you are a good and faithful servant upon getting to heaven?

Is it how to avoid hell?

Is it the fear of death?

Is it the disagreement in the Organisation of Petroleum Exporting Countries?

Is it the balance of trade and payment problems?

Is it the threat of a nuclear holocaust?

No!

I can say that the most urgent problem confronting you as a born-again Christian is not a place in heaven when your service on earth is over. You have a sure witness in your spirit that your faith in Jesus Christ of Nazareth as your Saviour and Lord gives you a definite guarantee that your eternal destiny will be with God.

Local, national and international matters are important to you, doubtless, but we can agree that they are not the salient issues of your daily life.

It stands to reason that the most vital and crucial question facing you is *How can you muster faith to overcome life's storms while you live on earth on your way to heaven*?

My heart goes out to thousands of people who write to me week after week throughout the year. These are men and women in the universities, businesses, construction companies, diplomatic services, the armed forces, and the police services. Everyone of them without exception writes to enquire, 'How can I overcome this storm raging around me?'

Some cry bitterly, 'Why should this happen to my family? What have I done that I must go through this painful ordeal?'

These questions only give rise to agony and in no small way increase their frustration.

A storm of life often comes upon us when it is least expected. If you had anticipated it, maybe you would have taken some preliminary measures to offset it. But now, here it comes unceremoniously!

Maybe your boss sends you a dismissal letter. Maybe your landlord increases the rent by one hundred percent.

Maybe your loved one is lost in an accident. Maybe your children are thrown out of school in the middle of the month. Maybe your only car breaks down prior to an urgent journey.

Maybe a family member has been hospitalised for a major operation. Maybe the family budget has exceeded the net income. Maybe divorce is staring you in the face.

Maybe one or more of these befall you. You are hurting, you can't sleep. Life is not worth living in your estimation.

'I'm scared and need urgent help. Who can help me? Who will share my burden with me? Does God's word provide an answer for life's storms? Can God get me over . . . at least this once?'

Any of the things I have outlined can become a storm in your life. This is the reality of life here on earth, not the heaven we are going to someday.

People write to us about their problems, fears and hurts. These letters touch my heart in no small way because I have been through it before. A man gave me a letter in London once. It said, 'My questions are endless. My mind cannot lay hold of a solution. Nobody seems to have the answer. Sleep has fled. I am more depressed because all my friends have left me. Much as I try to put on a cheery attitude, my depression shows through. Archbishop, my wife and children are discouraged. Alcohol has compounded my problems; I fear being addicted.'

This man was once a top business executive in London. In the last part of his letter he asks, 'Is there a way out?'

There is a way out of the problem. A way out of the storm. Wipe the tears out of your eyes. Open your heart to what God will direct you to do and by your obedience, all will be history.

The Bible gives us a broad perspective of a storm-hit life, its effect and the scriptural principles for dealing with it, as we will discover from the experience of the twelve apostles, in Matthew 14:22–24.

> And straightway Jesus constrained his disciples to get into a ship, and to go before him unto the other side, while he sent the multitudes away.
>
> And when he had sent the multitudes away, he went up into a mountain apart to pray: and when the evening was come, he was there alone.
>
> But the ship was now in the midst of the sea, tossed with waves: for the wind was contrary.

The Bible makes no secret of the fact that the disciples were acting on the Master's instructions to go over to the other side. Under normal circumstances if they were acting in disobedience against the express will of Jesus Christ, then maybe you would think their crisis was understandable.

But can you imagine it? A storm overtakes the disciples of Jesus? Yes, that is what the Bible says. It will help you if I bare my heart and disclose this point to you at this moment. Accepting it may not be easy, but it is a matter of time before you will appreciate the depth and wisdom underlying it all.

People in every society I have visited ask *why* to several things that befall them. Candidly, I can say you probably do, too. In all frankness, we can predict that

maybe the twelve disciples also had good reason to ask
why.

Why then?

The storm came unexpectedly upon them. It came as
suddenly as it comes upon our lives at times. Panic
broke out on board.

Twelve disciples travelling in obedience.

Twelve disciples carrying out the Master's orders.

Twelve disciples going over to the other side.

The *why*s will creep in upon you with a stifling
intensity.

Let one thing control your mind if you are a child
of God — Jesus knows something about the situation
you are going through that you don't know.

Also bear in mind that you don't have to do anything
wrong for some of the storms of life to hit you as it
did the disciples.

Two cardinal factors should uphold your heart in
the storm:

God will help you to succeed. Satan will help you
to fail.

God will not help you to fail. Satan will not help
you to succeed.

One of my dear mentors in the ministry, Dr Oral
Roberts, puts it this way,

> The two threads running through the Bible and all of life
> on Earth are, first, God seeking to bless and guide men
> — that's you too, you know — whom He created in His
> own likeness; and second, the devil seeking to change
> you from the way God made you so he can lead you astray

and destroy you. These are the two threads. Everything hangs on them.

From Matthew 14:22 we can infer that if the twelve disciples had not undertaken to go 'over to the other side' and had just stayed where they were, no storm would have hit them. But what you must also realise is that the other side is where new horizons exist.

The other side is where new opportunities exist.

The other side is where you break new ground.

The other side is a place of refreshment.

The other side is a celebration of victory.

The other side is a new way of life . . . from glory to glory.

Dr Oral Roberts has made a monumental contribution by God's grace to Christian testimony in a way only few preachers can equal. There is common agreement that Dr Roberts has seen persecution and gone through storms of life in dimensions far too alarming for many to comprehend.

He has asked many, many *why*s!

Several years ago, God dropped a deep revelation in his heart. This is a sound revelation which will open your spirit to the deeper understanding of divine operation in your life.

God said to him, 'I am trying to get man to the *other side*! Because man chose to run his own life through his physical senses instead of through his spirit, even the elements have been changed. Everything is upset and out of order. By man's ability to handle life's situations through his intellect, he has brought upon himself wars, murders, violence, perversion, and a terrible darkness over his inner self. Sickness strikes him. Death overtakes him. Everywhere he turns, he faces problems and needs he cannot cope with.

'He has poisoned the earth and the atmosphere by too often taking the wrong kind of dominion, a kind that leaves God out. He has poisoned his mind and body by denying his spirit its proper place in his life. He has put his spirit down and put his mind in charge. This is a reversal of the order in which I made him to function as a whole person. Because man chose to respond through his intellect and five senses rather than his spirit first, there are storms and struggles in the way of getting to the other side. Any direction he takes, good or bad, he runs into storms, into struggles that seek to destroy him.'

The words God spoke to Dr Roberts, quoted above, are a fundamental key to your new understanding of the *why*s of life's storms. Read it again with your spirit and see the wisdom of God beyond the mind's ability to grasp.

From this day, let the *why*s be settled once and for all. Millions of people never graduate from the school of self-pity and never learn anything beyond asking *why*, year after year. This is the devil's trump card. Leave the *why*s behind you. Go on!

You will achieve success by using the new truths and revelations in this book if you feel a firm response first with your spirit, your inner man of the heart.

For years I tried to reason it out. Beloved friend, I tell you the truth, I failed woefully. Each time I was baffled with the *why*s and feasted my mind on them.

One of the Greek words for 'word' is *sperma*. God's word is the seed of reproduction. When it comes forth it reproduces life, faith, power, new birth and healing. His word will not come forth in power or reproduction unless you do away with unbelief and religious indoctrination. Let these words produce a force of faith within you now.

I do not consider myself special—far from it. My struggles are frighteningly real, sometimes devastating, as I strive to go to the other side. The secret I have learned over the years is to originate my response to the storms *in my spirit*.

The wheelbarrow man

After the historic Fire Conference, organised by German evangelist Reinhard Bonnke in Zimbabwe, one of our Bible school graduates from Zambia came over to me and said, 'Archbishop, please come over to my country and hold a crusade.'

Later, in 1986, Rev. Lawrence Mwamba flew to Benin City and finalised arrangements for a national healing crusade from September 23–27, 1988, at the Kulima Tower Car Park in the heart of Lusaka.

For months, advertisements for the crusade were broadcast on television and radio. Large posters and handbills seemed to be everywhere on the streets of Lusaka. Full page newspaper ads appeared almost every two weeks.

The news of the historic crusade spread like a prairie fire over the countryside. People from the city carried the news by word of mouth to the most remote areas of Lusaka. The nation was set for what was indeed a divine appointment for the nation of Zambia.

'Papa' (we shall call him that out of respect for his age) had been a successful businessman. He had seen the best life could offer. Many of his children occupied top managerial positions in his nation. Following his retirement from a middle-executive job, Papa settled down among his people in the countryside.

One day, Papa complained about dizziness and bodily pains. Everyone thought it was one of the bodily changes associated with senility. But that was not the case. For weeks Papa grew weaker and medical attention from the local clinic did not seem to help much.

Papa began to spend huge sums of money to find an answer to his failing health. In a matter of months, his condition worsened as he was struck with paralysis.

'Let's take Papa to one of the modern hospitals in Lusaka. Maybe they can help,' someone kindly suggested.

Friend, this is a storm of life for which Papa had not bargained.

As the hospital bills increased, all his friends, and even his children, abandoned Papa. The hospital threatened to evict Papa if he did not take steps to settle his mounting bills.

Then came our World Outreach Crusade to Lusaka. Some whispered to Papa, 'There will be a healing crusade not far from here. Would you like to attend? Maybe something will happen.'

Papa had never been to church. 'My friend,' he said tearfully to the good news bearer, 'you know I have never been to church and I don't know what this Jesus thing is all about.'

'You can find out if you don't mind. It's worth a try,' the young man said encouragingly.

Papa stared through the window and said blankly, 'Young man, you know I don't have a car to take me there even if I decide to go, since I cannot walk.'

'If you agree to go, I will look for a friend's car to give you a lift,' the young man replied forcefully.

Papa did not say a word to that. The young man left the hospital after providing Papa with detailed instructions on the crusade time and when he hoped to come with the car to take him to the field.

Papa was caught between self-pity, tears, and confusion. He reflected on the 'good old days' and the 'bad new days'. Papa had been hard hit by a storm of life and a devastating one which had rendered him paralysed.

Dare to do

The whole night Papa could not sleep one minute. Various images danced in his mind. 'Am I going to die like this?' he said out loud. Everywhere was silent in the hospital ward, except for the cry of owls and chattering of crickets.

What a pleasant relief it was for Papa as the first rays of morning light broke out through the window panes.

Life went on as usual until three p.m. The young man rushed into the hospital ward and hurried to Papa's bed.

'Papa, Papa,' he called frantically, 'I could not get my friend's car and no taxi is willing to come over here.'

Papa asked mournfully, 'What are we going to do?'

'We will go, by all means. The crusade field is just over there,' he said, pointing a little distance to where local gospel singing was emanating.

Papa questioned uncertainly, 'How can we go?'

After a momentary silence, the young man replied, 'Papa, if nothing else works, I will take you to the crusade field in that wheelbarrow standing there.'

Papa blinked a couple of times and tears flowed freely from his eyes. It was all like a dream. But it was a storm of life and he must muster faith to overcome it.

After much persuasion, a male nurse helped the young man to carry Papa into the green wheelbarrow for the painful journey to the crusade field.

'It is too hard to sit inside this wheelbarrow. Please put clothing in it for some comfort,' Papa pleaded.

The journey started in earnest. Papa could not believe his eyes. It was like a dream. Maybe a drama or a play. Maybe an apparition or something, but it was real!

Everyone turned to look at the young man and the wheelbarrow man. 'What is this? What a shame,' a few sneered as the young man pushed the wheelbarrow to the edge of the crusade platform.

For every storm there is a calming voice

From the platform, my eyes followed the wheelbarrow to where the young man stopped at the edge of the platform. Then God said to me in my spirit, 'My servant, the wheelbarrow man is here on divine appointment. I shall raise him from his deathbed and calm his storm today.'

The moment I started to preach, I called the attention of the crowd to the poor state of the wheelbarrow man and God's promise of healing. The crowd shouted with excitement. It was a singular night of thousands surrendering to Christ as Saviour and Lord.

When the time came to minister healing to the sick, I asked the young man to push the wheelbarrow onto the platform for the thousands of people to see.

By the anointing of the Spirit of God and in the name of Jesus, I commanded the wheelbarrow man to stand up. The power of God moved into play. Gradually, with wobbling feet, the wheelbarrow man stood up. The crowd roared in overwhelming praise to God. With the systematic calculations of a toddler, the wheelbarrow man took one giant step towards me. Then another one . . . he increased his strides . . . then gathered speed . . . suddenly he flew into my arms. The paralysis was gone. Healing had come!

The wheelbarrow man wept! The crowd cried out with tears of joy! My eyes were heavy with tears of unconcealed happiness.

Pulling himself together, the wheelbarrow man shared his harrowing story. The storm came, but the beauty of the story is that God would not let that man down.

Friend, storms of life are real and so is God's calming power.

Always remember and never lose sight of this fact: *When you don't know what to do in the storm or the hour of distress — God knows what to do*.

Jesus knows you exist.

Jesus cares about you.

Jesus knows just what you are going through.

Jesus will stand by you in the storms of life.

As you read this book, a new way of life is opening up before you. From this day onwards, no storm need overcome you. New ideas for breakthrough will fill your mind. A fresh, new attitude of success can overflow your soul today.

The greatest insurance on earth, my dear friend, is to get hooked up with God.

The good news is — you simply cannot fail when he is your partner.

2

Dealing with Discouragement

It is not hard to detect that the whole world is searching for a purpose in living. Millions are seeking the reality of God. Multiplied millions are craving for tangible evidence that the Bible is true — and if so, how to make a fool-proof practical application of the divine injunctions in it to an individual life.

Millions on this earth have simply resigned themselves to some blind fate: 'What is to be, will be, and nothing can alter it.'

In this negative stance, teeming millions have surrendered their faith altogether, relegating God, Jesus Christ, and the Holy Bible to the position of a primitive or medieval indoctrination.

Religious dogmas program society to believe tenaciously that God is far too complex and mysterious for man to relate to.

How then do you explain Matthew 11:28? 'Come unto me, all ye that labour and are heavy laden, and I will give you rest.'

It says God is asking men and women with burdens to come into his open arms and find rest.

The business world believes in solving its problems. The politicians do not run out of new ideas for crisis-ridden society. But if there is a problem in your relationship with God, my friend, listen, God's word gives the answer.

Do you know that when faith in God is repudiated, people lose faith in society, in other people, and in no time, *in themselves*? They become purposeless, restless, and pursue life without aim, fulfilment, or direction.

Can you explain the high level of lawlessness, murder, iniquity, and even suicide which bedevil our society today? Millions are displeased, pent up with disillusionment of society and themselves. Because they cannot find a way to overcome the storms of life, they release the storm upon society.

You will not be amazed by what a great American evangelist said: 'People are at war with themselves. Emotional and psychological disturbances destroy a greater percentage of people than ever before. A psychiatrist at the world-famous John Hopkins Hospital reported that sixty percent of the patients there require mental and spiritual treatment, rather than physical.'

Instead of seeing the storms through your financial upsets, marital problems, business upheavals, depression, and living vulnerably to every physical plague that ravages human beings, discover that *God has become your companion for victory through life's adversities*.

God has a plan mapped out for your life. Hebrews

13:5 declares, '. . . for he hath said, I will never leave thee, nor forsake thee.'

Jesus Christ himself assured the disciples, '. . . and lo, I am with you alway, even unto the end of the world' (Mark 28:20). 'Alway' speaks of a daily, permanent presence of Jesus Christ in every circumstance, situation, or crisis. Whichever way things turn out, his committed promise is that he will be there with you in it all.

You were not made by God to walk life's pathway all by yourself. You were not made to walk alone. As Dr T.L. Osborn said about life's pathway, 'There are wild mountains scarred by deep ravines and gulches. There are rampaging rivers, avalanches, slides, difficulties, enemies that raid the sheep, chilling storms, and innumerable hazards.'

All these are true. All these are storms of life. But the greater truth is that the Good Shepherd knows every single pitfall and danger. There is great consolation in the words of Hebrews 4:15:

> For we have not an high priest which cannot be touched with the feeling of our infirmities; but was in all points tempted like as we are, yet without sin.

My dear friend, let your heart be at peace this day. You are not in this trial alone. You are not in the storm alone. Let not your soul be cast down within you.

Jesus Christ has passed this way before. He is the Calmer of the turbulent storm. He is the Walker on the violent waters. He is going with you through the disappointments, the broken dreams, and shattered hopes.

I have come to think that it pleases God for you to interrupt him with your cries and needs.

Let your heart rejoice because you can reach out and touch God in the depth of your agony, in the silence of your life, in your hurting emotions.

Someone said, 'But God is so busy running the universe.' Let me tell you this open secret, 'Yes, God is busy . . . but his business is you.'

The Chief Shepherd

The Twenty-third Psalm has had a whole religion made out of it. Almost any kindergarten child who has seen the inside of a church or read the Bible before can recite it with proficiency. Adults in mainline historic churches will not be outdone by their children. They print Psalm 23 on leaflets and hang them by their beds. It is everyone's favourite.

But, in spite of all these empty religious displays, the depth and beauty of this glorious psalm touches my spirit every time I read or preach on it. It is my fervent prayer that as I share some new insights about Psalm 23 with you that the eyes of your understanding and your spirit will be enlightened. I can tell you, you can make more spiritual progress in a few days and months than you can in twenty years of studying the Bible if you act on these principles by faith.

'The Lord is my shepherd.' This is an unflinching hint that assures mortal man that he is the object of divine diligence. I believe this thought alone should be enough to provide the desired energy the Christian needs on a daily basis to cope with all that life presents.

'I shall not want.' Does this verse mean that King David always had everything he wanted? Of course not! This does not refer only to material things. When David said these great words, he was saying that since he knew he had the best Shepherd of all, he could completely trust his present and future life into his Shepherd's hands.

'He leadeth me in the paths of righteousness for his name's sake.' It is very easy to tell what kind of shepherd a man is by looking at the condition of his pastures.

Christ, the Good Shepherd, will lead you beside the still waters.

Religious faith is not transmitted genetically. It is a satisfying experience when the 'Faith of our fathers' becomes more than just a song or sentiment and confidently becomes, 'My faith looks up to Thee.'

David knew the calm confidence of God's protection when the bear and the lion came. When he faced Goliath he knew he was on good ground because Jehovah was there.

David was a man who schooled himself in the mechanics of triumphing where others flopped. Every major crisis brought him to the point of making serious re-evaluations of his life in relationship to God. His secret was that nothing stopped him from going forward or outlasting the storm.

When the storm of life hits you, I can assure you the next thing to expect is discouragement.

Beloved, listen to my word, give no place to discouragement, no matter what happens in your life. You cannot afford to stop too long to lament the opportunities you've forfeited and cry over spilt milk. Put the pieces together and get going!

Walter Pope Binns, the late president of William Jewell College, is known to have preached a notable sermon at the college each year entitled, 'Irreparable Past — Available Future.'

He said the storms of life often fill us with regret of the past to the point where we cringe and despair.

I love how Walter Pope Binns looks at it all: 'But God's person has another dimension of life to explore. That dimension is the new opportunity that God gives — the open door to the future. God can forgive and redeem the past. He can give insight, strength, and new hope for the future.'

When the unexpected happens

We are going to examine critically a classic example from the Bible and the life of the beloved servant of God, a biblical foundation on how you react constructively when the storm hits you unexpectedly.

Do you opt to go under? Do you fizzle out in despair? Is it a case of complete surrender like a sitting duck? If an integral part of life's storms is discouragement, then it behooves you to learn all you can about it.

First Samuel 30:3–10 says:

> So David and his men came to the city, and, behold, it was burned with fire; and their wives, and their sons, and their daughters, were taken captives.
> Then David and the people that were with him lifted up their voice and wept, until they had no more power to weep.

And David's two wives were taken captives, Ahinoam the Jezreelitess, and Abigail the wife of Nabal the Carmelite.

And David was greatly distressed; for the people spake of stoning him, because the soul of all the people was grieved, every man for his sons and for his daughters: but David encouraged himself in the Lord his God.

And David said to Abiathar the priest, Ahimelech's son, I pray thee, bring me hither the ephod. And Abiathar brought thither the ephod to David.

And David inquired at the Lord, saying, Shall I pursue after this troop? Shall I overtake them? And he answered him, Pursue: for thou shalt surely overtake them, and without fail recover all.

So David went, he and six hundred men that were with him, and came to the brook Besor, where those that were left behind stayed.

But David pursued, he and four hundred men: for two hundred abode behind, which were so faint that they could not go over the brook Besor.

From an academic perspective we can categorise the principles in these verses under crisis management. But on a spiritual plane, we are dealing with far deeper things of life which are more than crisis management. In actual fact, it will be safer to say it takes absolute control to get rid of the problem in the name of Jesus Christ of Nazareth.

The account we just read in 1 Samuel 30:3–10 indicates that David and his men were on a military campaign elsewhere when the Amalekites struck their home base and took the women and children captive. David had not called for it. David did not provoke the Amalekites. David did not expect the attack. We can say this was a storm in David's life. Many *why*s erupted in David's mind. The enemy had done their worst.

In verse two, we read that when David and his men returned to Ziklag, they found the place in desolation, with their wives and children all gone. What tragedy! The sad aspect, in verse four, is what I will not recommend to you as a remedial measure when the storm of life comes calling.

David and all his soldiers wept aloud. The Bible says, 'Then David and the people that were with him lifted up their voice and wept, until they had no more power to weep.' You might ask whether the weeping brought back the captives. Since it did not, I can say it was a sheer waste of energy. The vital energy which was wastefully expended in the marathon weeping session could have been converted into strength to chase after the enemy.

My friend, if the enemy can get you to throw your hands up in distress and weep when the storm comes, he has got you.

Weeping in the hour of crisis introduces a chapter of discouragement and division in your camp. In verse six, you read that after all the weeping, 'the people spake of stoning him.'

What were they going to stone him for? They had lost their sense of direction and their vision was blurred with tears. The battle they had forgotten was a spiritual one and unwarranted tears placed them on an emotional level of operation.

Take a serious look at the last part of verse six, 'but David encouraged himself in the Lord his God.'

Do you see something strange in the verse? It was

only David who encouraged himself in the Lord his God. What do you think the crying gang was doing? You can guess!

Thank God, David had sense enough to stop weeping after a while. He got out of his fear and discouragement and into faith to pursue the enemy. David moved from walking in the flesh into the realm of spiritual understanding.

In the book of Daniel 11:32 it says, '. . . but the people that do know their God shall be strong, and do exploits.' We can now say of David that he knew his God and that's the reason why he did exploits.

My friend, the number one principle when the unexpected happens in your life is to *encourage yourself in the Lord your God*. Don't ever forget this. It is the dividing line between life and death, going over and going under, and defeat or success. The choice is yours.

What a man David was! It is not at all surprising that the Bible says he was a man after God's heart. He called for the ephod and enquired from the Lord.

What lessons do you learn from David? Your greatest undoing is to say his method is archaic and old-fashioned or maybe an Old Testament style. David called for the ephod. In today's terminology, he called for his Bible.

Who do you enquire from when the storm hits you? Do you go rushing down to your unbelieving friends? Do you pray about it? Do you find out what God's mind is before you embark on any course of action?

The second principle is that *David enquired of the Lord*. The Bible has an answer for every human need.

Your crisis or problem is not exempt. Find out what God has specifically said. If you are in doubt, consult your pastor or seek counsel from a spiritually sound and mature Christian leader.

You should have a spirit of knowing to enable you to have a spirit of winning in life. So know God and win your wars.

God does not give choices, he gives instructions. He told David to pursue the enemy. It was up to David to go or stay. The Bible says David moved into action. The man who walks by faith has a one-track mind. He understands nothing else but victory.

Faith brings God on the scene. Act accordingly, because the fight you are in is a faith fight. Believe God's word!

The third principle is that David *was courageous*. If you win inside you, you will conquer outside. If you read carefully Joshua, chapter one, it will surprise you how many times God Almighty admonished him to be strong and courageous. I cannot open your mouth and breathe courage into you. Courage is an action word. God told Joshua to be courageous and put on the spirit of courage. Courage comes from a deep knowing in the depths of your heart that God's word is true in any situation.

When courage comes, panic flees through the window. The Bible proclaims that the righteous shall be as bold as lions; that speaks of courage in the face of stormy situations.

Beloved, you can have faith to recover your possessions. Put off discouragement when the storms come. Put on courage and stand eyeball to eyeball with the devil.

You want to walk by faith? Then I charge you to be courageous.

In 1 Samuel 30:11–12 we read:

And they found an Egyptian in the field, and brought him to David, and gave him bread and he did eat; and they made him drink water;

And they gave him a piece of a cake of figs, and two chisters of raisins: and when he had eaten, his spirit came again to him . . .

In the same way 1 Corinthians 10:13 promises that with every temptation God makes a way of escape. David also found out that in every crisis or storm of life, God provides an avenue of relief or opportunity to tide you over.

David and his men found a boy abandoned by the rampaging army. I believe God had a hand in the boy's abandonment to give David a guide. So it is that even in the heat of it all, God will give you a word of prophecy, a word of wisdom, or human support of one kind or another to stem the tide of the enemy against you.

The Scriptures exhort us to 'be wise as serpents, and harmless as doves' (Mt 10:16). God enjoins us to feed our enemies and it worked miracles for David when he obeyed the divine injunction. Never shift your ground one bit from the word of God no matter what comes your way. The way through the storm is by the way of the word.

And so we can say the fourth principle when the unexpected happens is to *help others in weaker situations*. If you are spiritual and word-conscious, I bet chances are that there will always be thousands of people who need your help regardless of your distress. Minister to someone in a weaker position. Remember, God has said: 'Let the strong help the weak.'

Any time I read Job 42:10, it refreshes my heart. It says, 'And the Lord turned the captivity of Job, when he prayed for his friends: also the Lord gave Job twice as much as he had before.'

This Scripture verse should mean something to you and minister grace to your spirit.

Job was hit by a crisis. We can say it was a storm of life. It was also unexpected. Few men born of women can stand what Job endured, but thanks be to God who can make all grace to abound toward us.

I believe Job suffered serious discouragement from his close associates and even his wife, who advised him to curse God and die (Job 2:9). In the heat of his affliction, Job turned his eyes away from the storm and the struggles. He prayed for his detractors and that was a seed which bore fruit in the miracle of a double portion of blessing.

You can also do the same, can't you? Say you can! Don't hold a grudge against anyone who contributed to the crisis or storm you are in now. Forgive and forget.

By God's enabling grace, David and his team recovered all their wives and property. What do I see out of this, in your situation? I am bold to say to you, come hell and come high water, not one piece of hair on your head will be lost to the enemy. Everything happening around you will count for a testimony in the days coming.

After the recovery of lives and property, something significant happened we must not ignore.

1 Samuel 30:23, 24, says, 'Then said David, Ye shall not do so, my brethren, with that which the Lord hath given us, who hath preserved us, and delivered the company that came against us into our hand.

'For who will hearken unto you in this matter? But as his part is that goeth down to the battle, so shall his part be that tarrieth by the stuff: they shall part alike.'

The fifth principle you must cultivate when the storm or crisis is over is *share your success with others*. David did not have a grabbing spirit of covetousness. He put the pain of the crisis behind him and established a new foundation of mutual trust and love.

Give God your promise that you will allow the principles outlined in this chapter to build a solid bedrock of faith which can withstand pressure, trial, and crisis.

Is discouragement normal?

Your point of dire need or crisis hour is not the only time God may appear in some form to help you. God is sovereign and can and does appear as he wills.

When the storms of life come, God expects you to do your part. If you don't then discouragement sets in because you misjudged his timing.

At times you expect him to appear to you in the moment of crisis. After the counsel of his own will, if he doesn't by your timing discouragement floods your heart. You don't have to allow discouragement under any circumstance in your Christian experience; it will weaken the foundation of your faith more than anything else.

Soon you will look to that dreadful hour when you thought all the world had come to an end. New vistas of hope and testimony will open up before you with strong experiences, to withstand similar trials along the way.

Let me kindly share this interesting story with you. I heard a preacher use it to illustrate a point in his sermon and it seems to fit into the point I am establishing here.

The evangelist said one day the devil held a trade fair and put various items and goods on display at give-away prices. Common among the goods on conspicuous display were sin, unrighteousness, fear, sickness, and everything else you can imagine Satan putting on sale.

The evangelist elaborated further that after what looked like bonanza sales for the devil, there was just one single sale, and that was *discouragement*.

On a funny note the evangelist asked the devil why he would not sell discouragement, and the devil answered, 'It is the most precious commodity in my arsenal. When a man becomes discouraged, he begins to doubt the promises of God. A discouraged person loses his sense of direction and is bogged down in self-pity and doubt.'

This short story may not be exactly scriptural, but carries a deep revelation of satanic operation as shown in the word of God. Various instances in both the Old and New Testament show expressly that a child of God could be discouraged. You could be discouraged, but you have to be a Christian believer, no matter the storms of life which confront you.

Among Christian leadership, discouragement is a death trap. In one of his books Dr Billy Graham speaks of discouragement.

> Discouragement is nothing new. It is as old as man. It comes many times when we don't get our own way, when things don't work out the way we want them to.
>
> Discouragement is the very opposite of faith. It is Satan's device to thwart the work of God in our lives.
>
> Discouragement blinds our eyes to the mercy of God and makes us perceive only unfavourable circumstances.

Dr Graham has walked with God long enough to know what he is saying and I pray you to take his words seriously.

Someone said the Christian's chief occupational hazards are depression and discouragement.

According to Alan Langstaff, 'Discouragement comes following a great defeat or disappointment in our lives . . . it will often come halfway through a task . . . When the job is halfway through, there is the temptation to think *We'll never get there, we'll never get it finished!* Discouragement can often come following a victory or an achievement.'

Alan Langstaff observed that discouragement can be caused by overload (Num 11:10–15), defeat (Josh 6:6–9), apparent failure (1 Kings 19:4), poor health (Is 38), opposition (Neh 6), and divine opposition (Acts 16:6).

No place for discouragement

The saddest ploy you can fall into is to allow discouragement to drag on indefinitely. It will lead to confusion, consequent loss of vision, and withdrawal or backslidden spirit.

Discouragement, by its nature, will just not fizzle out into thin air as you would have wished. No, not discouragement. Besides, it is highly contagious.

Encouragement comes from the Lord and so we can tell where discouragement shoots out from — Satan.

Please keep your eye on the Lord and the vision he has given you in spite of the storm. Make no room for discouragement. You can pray it out. Sometimes depression seizes you and in such situations, simply pray in the spirit until the peace of God floods your innermost being.

You can persevere, endure, and stand. Exercise your faith in the promises of God. If you cannot stand the tide all alone, it is not a sin to ask brethren to support you in prayers (Gal 6:2).

Be blessed by the words of encouragement Dr Oral Roberts penned which he labelled a formula for success:

> I will do what I can do.
> Then I will expect God to do what he can do.
> I will not ask God to do what I can do.
> I will not try to do what only he can do.
> I will get a new relationship with God as my miracle partner and we will do what we can do together.
> I will expect the good from what I can do.
> I will expect the miracle that God can do.
> I will expect a miracle.
> I will *expect miracle after miracle!*

Thousands of Christian believers, as well as unbelievers, say to me, 'Do you ever get discouraged with what you do?' I respond: 'Discouragement is the lot of mortal man. I respond to it by listening to God rather than men. They are moments of sober reflection.'

In times like that my wife Margaret will look at me and say, 'This is just for a passing moment. It will soon be over. You will outlive the discouragement.' And so we have.

Preachers and believers all over the world are keenly watching my life of faith and utterances as a leader. Any sign of visible discouragement will cause ripples far and wide. What then do I do? I normally take a course Satan would never envision. I go to the All Nations for Christ Bible Institute and preach on the promises of God. It fires my spirit. I look for something new to do for Christ. The things that I preach to others I begin to preach to myself.

Let me make this abundantly clear to you today. There is not and never will be such a thing as winning a one-time total victory over the devil in this mortal life. Disabuse your mind of such a notion.

Discouragement will come in the storms of life. Don't let it possess you. Worse still, a sad countenance will ruin the beauty of God's glory in you.

You can't be human and not be discouraged. Day and night, by his grace, I labour for the kingdom of God. Naturally, I expect someone to pat me on the back and say, 'Benson Idahosa, that is great of you. Keep up the pace. We believe in what you are doing.'

Friend, I am afraid to say that often the voice of

encouragement will be silent and the whispers of discouragement will bound aloud. Many will confront you: 'Who do you think you are? Anybody else can do what you are doing. You can quit if you want.'

Be blessed to hear this. The sign of the winner is, 'How am I going to get out of this?' The sign of a loser is, 'Why did God let this happen?'

Get this straight in your head. Stand for God no matter what happens in this life.

I made up my mind decades ago I am going to serve God whether in sickness or health, happy or unhappy, poor or rich. In success or failure, I am sold out for God. I belong to him. When I am discouraged and when the victory comes we are an unbeatable team. The goodness is that God has put me on the winning side and nothing will take away my joy of salvation.

Let me finally tell you something Jesus Christ will unfailingly tell you when he meets a person in a crisis, problem, or storm of life.

He says, 'Be of good cheer!'

3

The Word of God Rules the Storm

Someone made a cursory overview of Christianity and said that the Christian life is not difficult, *it is impossible*! Some strong truths lay hidden in this statement, because none of us can live a Christian life in our own strength. However, I have confidence to say that with the power that comes to us at salvation, we can do all things through Christ who strengthens us (Phil 4:13).

Beyond doubt, because of this power working in us, the Christian life can be victorious every day, rather than dreary patches of trial and error.

Karl Strader captures the mood of what I am saying by his statement: 'But to be victorious, there are two areas that all Christians need strength in — tests and battles. Tests have to do with our everyday living experiences. Battles are with the evil side of the unseen world — Satan's world, the world of darkness.'

If any man faced crises and storms of life because of the gospel, you can count the apostle Paul among them. A glance at 2 Corinthians, chapter 11 will give you an idea of what I mean.

Some extensive Scripture references from Acts 27 will help us to see the place of God's word in the heat, pressures, and storms of life:

> And when it was determined that we should sail into Italy, they delivered Paul and certain other prisoners unto one man named Julius, a centurion of Augustus' band.
>
> And entering into a ship of Adramyttium, we launched, meaning to sail by the coasts of Asia; one Aristarchus, a Macedonian of Thessalonica, being with us (Acts 27:1,2).
>
> Now when much time was spent, and when sailing was now dangerous, because the fast was now already past, Paul admonished them,
>
> And said unto them, Sirs, I perceive that this voyage will be with hurt and much damage, not only of the lading and ship, but also of our lives.
>
> Nevertheless, the centurion believed the master and the owner of the ship, more than those things which were spoken by Paul (Acts 27:10,11).
>
> But after long abstinence Paul stood forth in the midst of them, and said, Sirs, ye should have hearkened unto me, and not have loosed from Crete, and to have gained this harm and loss.
>
> And now I exhort you to be of good cheer: for there shall be no loss of any man's life among you, but of the ship.
>
> For there stood by me this night the angel of God, whose I am, and whom I serve,
>
> Saying, Fear not, Paul; thou must be brought before Caesar: and, lo, God hath given thee all them that sail with thee.
>
> Wherefore, sirs, be of good cheer: for I believe God, that it shall be even as it was told me (Acts 27:21-25).

And when he had thus spoken, he took bread, and gave thanks to God in presence of them all: and when he had broken it, he began to eat.

Then were they all of good cheer, and they also took some meat (Acts 27:35,36).

I can count at my fingertips hundreds of Christians who feel on top of the world on Sunday, but are woefully depressed much of the week. On Monday, they are on a spiritual mountain top and on Wednesday, they are stressed out in the valley. Obviously, they don't have the strength to avoid this yo-yo Christian walk from mountain top to valley and back again, year after year.

A critical and impartial study of the life of Paul indicates that Satan did not give him much breathing space, but Paul had a testimony of standing when everything else fell around him. Paul had the prosperity of walking on the mountaintop spiritually while the valley of problems surrounded him.

The issue at stake is not whether or not the crisis or tests are our making or part of God's discipline. We generally agree that they are a part of a spiritual growing up process if we approach them in the light of God's word. Paul was by his life, message, and calling, the servant of God in no small measure. He had a testimony of faith and power. Before King Agrippa in Jerusalem, Paul testified about his faith in Jesus Christ. At the end of it all, Paul appealed that he be permitted to bring his case before a Roman king, Caesar, in Rome. There was no denying the fact that the hand of God was at work in Paul's ministry as seen in Acts 23:11: 'And the night following the Lord stood by him, and said, Be of good cheer, Paul: for as thou hast testified of me in Jerusalem, so must thou bear witness also at Rome.'

With divine assurance, the apostle Paul headed for Rome. The Bible says in verse 10 of Acts 27, that Paul warned, ' . . . Sirs, I perceived that this voyage will be with hurt and damage.' God, who was taking his servant to Rome, revealed something privately to him. Paul believed God's revelation and word. It is unfortunate the ship officials did not believe Paul. They did not know that aboard the ship was one of the greatest preachers of all time.

In verse 11, we see that the centurion believed the owner of the ship. But does that alter God's word? It doesn't.

Unbelief is believing anything outside God's word — the Bible calls it an evil report (Num 13).

When the storm of life comes you are not in it alone. Don't be afraid to say to men what the word of God says. Please don't believe what they believe — evil report. The Bible says, ' . . . stand still and see the salvation of the Lord . . .' (Exod 14:13).

The Bible declares, 'And call upon me in the day of trouble: I will deliver thee, and thou shalt glorify me' (Ps 50:15).

Let the world hear, 'He that dwelleth in the secret place of the most High shall abide under the shadow of the Almighty' (Ps 91:1).

Say to them, 'The name of the Lord is a strong tower: the righteous runneth into it, and is safe' (Prov 18:10).

Be bold enough to say, 'They that trust in the Lord shall be as mount Zion, which cannot be removed, but abideth for ever' (Ps 125:1).

Shout it out loud, 'No weapon that is formed against thee shall prosper; and every tongue that shall rise against thee in judgment thou shalt condemn. This is the heritage of the servants of the Lord, and their righteousness is of me, saith the Lord' (Is 54:17).

Paul was not a coward. A man of faith is not a coward. He told them what God had said. They chose not to believe. If they would not join Paul's faith, he was not willing to be part of their unbelief. The game of life is a spiritual one. Paul, like you, operated on a spiritual level far higher than natural circumstances.

Moments after Paul's divinely-inspired revelation about the storm which was debunked, a strong wind assailed them on every side. The seriousness of the situation is seen in Acts 27:15, which says they surrendered to the wind.

Did Paul jump into the sea? Of course not, I wouldn't expect him to. Did Paul cry mournfully because disaster was coming? No, because he knew in whom he had believed would also keep his word.

Did Paul attempt to commit suicide out of fear? No! The word of God was the foundation of his faith. I can say to you that even if heaven and earth pass away, God's word abides.

In this important chapter we are dealing with the place of God's word when the storms of life come crashing in upon you. There is so much we can also learn from Paul.

Would you have jumped into the sea in fear?

Would you have sided with the unbelieving ship owners?

Would you have cried out in unbelief?

Would you dare believe God's word in the face of overwhelming, contradictory, natural evidence?

Would you cast away your confidence and the due recompense of reward?

I adjure Paul on several grounds and here is one of them. In Acts 27:21 it says, ' . . . Paul stood forth in the midst of them, and said, Sirs, ye should have hearkened unto me . . .'

Paul was not invited to address the people on the ship, he stood up as led by the Spirit of God. In the eyes of everyone else on the ship, Paul was a common prisoner. But listen to me, that is not Paul's mind. From proceedings recorded in Acts 27:21–22, you can find out who was really in charge of affairs on board and dictating the pace. It was Paul. He may have been bound with chains on his hands, but his spirit was free, and that is where the orders came from.

We see Paul's gentle rebuke of the shipowner and captain in verse 21. A prisoner does not tell his boss, 'You should have listened to me.' Paul was not the officer in charge.

Maybe Paul beamed with a confident smile and said, ' . . . be of good cheer . . . for there stood by me this night, the angel of God, whose I am, and whom I serve' (Acts 27:22–23).

Paul did not hide his identity as some fearful Christians do today. Listen to him: 'I am not ashamed of the gospel of Christ . . .' (Rom 1:16).

If there is an opportune time to say you are a Christian who believes in Jesus Christ, it is when the storms of life emerge.

It is not hard to capture the spirit and mood on the

ship. None had eaten for over fourteen days. They were held captive between death and hopelessness. It was absolute bleakness. Discussions were going on how to kill the prisoners. Panic was reigning. Pandemonium held sway.

Then emerged a handbound prisoner against the whistling waves saying . . . 'be of good cheer . . . stood by me this night the angel of God . . . fear not.'

In verse 25, Paul summarised, 'Wherefore, sirs, be of good cheer: for I believe God, that it shall be even as it was told me.'

Read it again if you will. Paul was a believer. He did not make room in his heart for doubt and unbelief. If God said it, that is it! Let this posture be yours today. When storms arise, say, 'I believe God, that it shall be even as it was told me.'

The difference between going over and going under

There is a fear reigning in every country I have visited . . . an unexplainable spirit of fear and panic. People spend several hours discussing the economic recession. Others propound theories on inflation and its effects. Many are frantic and are almost at fever pitch about the high cost of living.

I once said, 'People fear so much they fear fear. Millions are worried about tomorrow. This wave of negativism gradually puts God on the outside or almost blotted out from their mouths.'

The Bible says that out of the abundance of the heart the mouth speaketh, or literally, the hand writes. (See Luke 6:45.) I feel fear in the letters of thousands who write to me. Some fear today, others tomorrow, and so on. It will highly surprise you to know some of these fearful and faithless people have gone bankrupt and have no jobs. Fear is no respecter of persons. Unbelief loves all men. In the face of all this avalanche of fear, what does God's word say? Whenever God comes on the scene, his maiden words are, 'Fear not.'

Someone has said that the Bible has 365 'fear nots', apparently one for each day of the year.

Faith is established upon God's word. Fear is established upon what the devil says, the dictates of our five physical senses and natural evidence. In Luke 1:74–75, the Lord assures us he will deliver us out of the hand of our enemies that we might serve him without fear all the days of our lives. A look at 2 Timothy 1:7, a favourite scripture of mine says, 'For God hath not given us the spirit of fear; but of power, and of love, and of a sound mind.'

If the Bible says that, where did we get fear from? I can say from believing Satan's lies.

My dear beloved, I want to make some serious statements at this point and you will be greatly helped if you accept them.

A whole lot of the crises and storms of life Christians or people of the world run into are self-inflicted.

Fear of the unknown will destroy you. Fear will cause you to make rash decisions contrary to the word of God.

Let me share with you a statement Dr Oral Roberts made which has been imprinted in my spirit for decades:

Your greatest source of supply and sense of security is in the things you lack, not in the things you have. For the things you have, if you are not careful, can become a god to you and you will lean on them. You might say, 'I have a good marriage, nothing will ever happen to it.' Or 'I have wonderful children, they will never go wrong. I am doing fine. I am okay, no matter what happens. I am okay!'

But when you do this you are leaning upon something of this world and God is left out. When we lean on material things — on our job, the money we have in the bank, etc, we lose something. We lose the sense of trust in God.

Ministry is people and ministry also takes money to run. Sincerely speaking, I never had enough money for ministry. We have large scale projects going on at various places. Churches are under construction in almost all the states of Nigeria. That takes faith, but you have to admit, it also takes money and much of it.

Every thirty days, salaries are due for payment. As the ministry expands, we hire more staff.

Talk about getting frantic! Talk about getting into storms of life on a daily basis! But where does it take me? To a place where I will bow my knees day and night to God and cry for help. I mean it, I have to tell God, 'Lord, you are in control, you are my supreme source. If you don't help me out, I'm grounded.

If you have ever thought of owning all the money in the world, listen to me: you would be the worse for it, because it would take away your sense of trust in God.

You've got to quit talking untruth and unbelief!
You've got to stick it out with the word of God!
You've got to doubt your doubts and believe God!
You've got to starve your doubts and feed your faith!

You've got to stand against the devil and quote the Bible!

You've got to stop mixing your faith with doubt!

You've got to listen to God's voice in the storm!

You've got to believe his word has the answers!

4

Faith Is a Way-Finder

Ye are of God, little children, and have overcome them:
because greater is he that is in you, than he that is in
the world (1 Jn 4:4).

For whatsoever is born of God overcometh the world:
and this is the *victory* that overcometh the world, even
our faith (1 Jn 5:4).

If there are verses you are in love with, my friend,
let these be two of them.

The Greater One indwells you. God in you is far
greater than Satan out there in the world. Promise me
you will remember this verse when adversities strike
your way.

'Are you asking that adversities come my way?' No,
that is not what I mean and I don't intend that you
misunderstand me. But if you want to know the truth,
adversities and storms of life will come somewhere and
sometimes without authorised invitation. Based upon
this sound understanding, wisdom dictates that you
put yourself in readiness for them, and that includes

firm knowledge that the Greater One (Jesus Christ) is in your heart to control affairs if you let him.

Faith is the victory. Thousands of pentecostal ministries all over the world have this phrase, *Faith Is the Victory*, as a slogan. You will agree that for millions of Christians there should be deep-seated knowing in the heart when crises shoot up that, indeed, faith is the victory!

Don't come to think that faith is the victory only when the sailing is smooth, but also when the water is rough.

A few months ago I visited a bookshop and my eyes took hold of a book sitting on the shelf. It was *Mountain-Moving Motivation*, by Karl Strader with Stephen Strang.

Gradually leafing through it, I read something which hit my spirit with revelation. He said,

> The only way the Christian life is possible, let alone easy, is by the Spirit and the power of God.
>
> Many people try, work, plod, and agonize in their own strength to live for Christ. How fruitless!
>
> It is never necessary for any Christian to have a blue day.
>
> It is never necessary for any Christian to be discouraged.
>
> It is never necessary for any Christian to be defeated.
>
> God wants his children to be on top of the mountain even when they are going through a valley. He wants them to have a song in the middle of the night.

Karl Strader made another remark:

> Problems? Sure, Christians will probably have more problems than sinners, because they are going against

the current of this world. But a Christian who relies on the Power of God flowing through him will never meet a problem with which he cannot cope or solve.

Christian believers who take their Lord seriously do not always impress others by great leaps forward. The fact is they refuse to take forbidden shortcuts. They plan the game of life by Christ's rules yet in the end, as it has always been proved, those who obey Christ are the true winners even if for a time they seem to be 'fools for Christ's sake' (1 Cor 4:10).

Aesop's fable of the tortoise and the hare makes a strong point, illustrating that the hare had such a resolute confidence in his own cleverness and swiftness that he was careless about how he ran the race. The tortoise, knowing his own limitations, developed a strategy and stayed with it. He consistently plodded on, never stopping, and passed the sleeping hare, thus winning the race. Paul said, 'Stand firm . . . in the Lord' (Phil 4:1).

Christian believers are often a source of wonder to unbelievers, by their testimony of faith and confession of life in the face of seeming defeat. And the reason is not hard to find. What you believe, whether you are aware or not, will ultimately affect your faith somewhere along the line.

A couple of years ago I read a book by Dr Kenneth Hagin titled *Right and Wrong Thinking*. In it I came across a strange statement. He said, 'People that think wrong believe wrong, and when they believe wrong, they act wrong.'

The words set off a ticking in my heart. I say it is a

strange remark because it upsets the religious doctrines of many churchgoers. If you would read what Dr Hagin said again, you will agree it is nothing but the truth in Scripture and Christian experience.

Your response to any particular situation which comes up in your life is understandably based upon premeditated knowledge, beliefs and values.

But the secret of faith is continually saying what God said. How are you going to know and say what God said when you don't know it? This is where the dangers lie for many Christians in our generation. They are plain, scriptural illiterates!

Many people write to me about how and why the word of God does not work for them. Foremost, I can say if you don't have time for God's word, it won't affect your life.

'But how do I find time for the word of God?' My answer to you is that, given quality time for meditation, the word will become part of you.

Let me say something crucial at this juncture. How strong, faith-filled and built on God's word you are will be known when the storm of life hits your boat.

The Bible says, 'Out of the abundance of the heart the mouth speaketh.' I have discovered that this is unusually true in the hour of need. Unconsciously you say something in that unguarded moment and it betrays your true foundation in God's word.

Under pressure it takes a 'spiritual knowing' of him whom you have believed, to stand and hold on to his word.

The commentary on the apostle Peter's life during

the last days of Jesus' ministry in Luke 22 will shed some light on what I mean.

You can hear the boasting of Peter to Jesus that he will never deny him. But Jesus was not convinced by Peter's impetuous and showy and shallow confessions.

Then the 'storm' came upon all the disciples and Peter was caught unaware and unprepared. It took only a young girl to show the world Peter's exact level of faith. Accusations came on Peter. The crowd yelled at him, 'You are a Jesus disciple!' Then the truth came out. Peter should have admitted knowledge of Jesus and probably would have been killed, too. Certainly, Jesus would not have loved it to be that way, but my point is that the whole setup indicates that the fisherman-turned-disciple still had a lot of the old nature at work. The word of Jesus Christ had not yet found a solid and unmovable foundation in his spirit.

When we review this incident in the light of what happened in Acts 5:29 where Peter said, ' . . . We ought to obey God rather than men,' we see a difference. Peter had meditated on the work of Jesus Christ and was more than willing to stake his life on it.

My counsel to you is that before the storm and crisis arise, feed your spirit with the word of God. Begin a process of training your spirit with the word of life. God's words are filled with faith and that is how faith comes.

Meditate on God's word

Remember, building up your inner man of the heart will never come by watching 'Midnight Blues' on television all night. Secondly, I must add that this vital process of training your spirit on the word of God is not an overnight dream. You will have discouragement from Satan. He knows if you have the word abundantly in your heart, his rulership and authority over you are broken.

Don't be misled into thinking, 'In a few weeks I will be full of faith.' Work at it with consistent commitment. Weed out all the religious trash and program your spirit with God's word.

Religion says that God deliberately brings the storms, sicknesses and crises to teach you a lesson. When I wasn't born again, I used to believe that junk, but salvation taught me that Satan comes to steal, kill and destroy. That is Satan's ministry!

God doesn't teach me anything through suffering: the Holy Spirit teaches me by God's word.

Someone will tell you, 'Oh, friend, don't worry, God gave you that fever to make you humble.' Do you agree? You will agree if you don't know God's word. But if you know the word, what do you do with that unbelief? You cast it down so you will not be defiled.

Tradition will tell you, 'If you feel sick, you are not healed.' The gospel says, 'By his stripes ye were healed' (1 Pet 2:24). When the storm of sickness comes, put your faith on this verse, and also Matthew 8:17. If you do, your faith will triumph over the works of evil.

Tradition and religion will try to convince you that if you pray and fast, and your problem worsens, keep bombarding the gates of heaven. Is that what God's word says? It says, 'When ye pray, believe that ye receive them, and ye shall have them' (Mk 11:24).

Believe for the answer *now*! Believe for the provision *now*!

The Bible says, '. . . and having done all, to stand. Stand therefore . . .' (Eph 6:13,14). You should know by now that whether you will stand or not depends on your faith. Faith in what? In God's word.

Wherever you talk about faith sometimes people get jittery and uncertain.

The Bible states, '. . . God hath dealt to every man the measure of faith' (Rom 12:3). First, not that God has given to every man a different measure, a variable quantity. It doesn't say God gave Dr T.L. Osborn more faith than to you. It doesn't say God loved me more and as a result gave me a greater measure of faith.

We all receive the same fixed measure of faith at salvation. There is no such thing as great faith, middle-sized faith, and little faith at salvation. You and I have the measure of God's own faith implanted in our spirit.

You want to ask, 'But how then is it that some great men of God have done mightier works than others if we all have the same measure of faith?'

This is a good question, and it demands a good answer. You can work on your measure of faith until it becomes great faith. How? That is what I want to share with you. Begin to use your measure of faith a lot of times, and that's all it takes to get you through the storm. Say with me now, 'I have enough to begin and that's all I need.'

Confess from your heart, 'I have enough faith to weather the storm and turn the tide in my favour by God's word.'

Now let us share this: 'I will act on what faith I have to believe with, and miracles will happen to me.'

Fear is far different from faith. Fear originates from your five senses (touch, hearing, tasting, smelling, and seeing). Thousands write to me, 'Why am I so afraid?' The simple answer is, 'Like most other people, you may be conducting your life by the directions your brain gets from what your eyes, ears, nose, tongue, and hands tell you, instead of following your spirit to tell you what to do.'

Faith says to keep our eyes steady, and of course, to let the word of God rule our heart.

'How can I get faith?' You will soon discover, as a Christian believer, that faith is not something you get. It is something you have. Walk in full knowledge of this fact that God has already given you faith. Exercise your faith and believe God.

Get me clearly on this count. Every storm that comes upon you, you have the faith to get over it. That sounds like a hard saying, but it's not.

The preacher might have told you before, 'Let your life count.' So I also urge you, 'Let your faith count.' The world screams, 'Seeing is believing,' but faith says, 'Believing is seeing.'

My friend, it is so much better being in close contact with God, trusting him, resting on him, living for him at all times. Then when the valley experiences come, you are not alone. There is so much faith build-up in your spirit that in such an hour, the storms only whistle past.

There certainly are times when we are highly impatient for our prayers to be answered, and I have come to know that should God heed some of our impatient begging, it would not be for our good. The faith that takes you through the 'valley experiences' is a patient faith.

A young man was begging God to give him a job. For a year, he had been knocking at office doors presenting his credentials, but no one seemed to welcome him with a smile. He could not understand. He was more qualified than many who managed to get the jobs. It was a bitter cycle of agony, and the pangs of unemployment and idleness hovered around him.

He set a deadline and earnestly begged God to answer his prayer. The day for an interview came. He prayed all night, 'Please, God, give me this job.'

But, lo and behold, he was refused, and he returned home in deep dejection and melancholy. Throughout the night, he was troubled in his spirit. The voice of the enemy came to him: 'Why not just commit suicide and end it all? After all, if God loved you, all this shame would not come your way.'

After much effort, he said a simple prayer and started out again the next morning to follow up other applications.

At the personnel manager's office he was told, 'Where have you been all these days? The general manager has been searching for you everywhere.'

The young man was lost for words. His mind whirled with various thoughts, and he said to himself, 'What can this mean?'

As he waited outside the door of the general manager's office, his heart pounded with anticipation. The giant wooden door swung open and he was ushered into the dignified presence of the general manager. 'Hello, young man. It is a joy to see you at last.' The general manager welcomed him to a comfortable chair.

'There is a job I have reserved for you in our marketing department,' the manager confided to the young man. He went on: 'Considering your impressive credentials, I am confident you can deliver the goods. Make arrangements and assume duty tomorrow. Pick up your appointment letter on your way home from the personnel department.'

The young man raced home to read the appointment letter. His eyes could not believe what he read. Twice as much pay as he had bargained for and fringe benefits beyond his expectation. He dropped the letter and bowed down on his knees praising the Lord.

Faith will always find a way. Faith will always tell you, 'God's supreme purpose in this whole episode is that when the chips are down, you will be better off.'

Oh, that you might realise that God knows more than you do and he wants the best for his children.

Only believe

When the nobleman 'heard that Jesus was come out of Judea into Galilee, he went unto him, and besought him that he would come down, and heal his son: for he was at the point of death. Then said Jesus unto him. Except ye see signs and wonders, ye will not believe' (Jn 4:47–48). Jesus made this statement more as an indictment on the man.

'You mean if there is no sign and wonder, you will not believe?' That is what the Lord was saying. The strong indication here is that most times you will have to believe simply by faith without the signs and wonders. How then do you do that? By relying on the word of God. There is a dynamic and living force in God's word to help you believe. The Bible is different from any other book on the face of the earth. It is vital and living.

Would you be surprised to hear this? Please don't be. The valley experiences and storms of life are not your problem. It is your believing.

When the Bible was written centuries ago, technology and advancement had not reached the level we are today. Men lived far simpler lives. Today, the television is a voice. Radio is an influence. Video wields power. Newspapers form opinions.

If, in those days of lesser societal influences, they were charged to stick closely to the word of God, our responsibility in this area is even greater. There is one sure thing to which we can anchor — the word of God.

I believe when we get to heaven many men will be astounded by the mind-storming importance of the word of God. Every phase of our Christian living points to the word.

All we know about God, Jesus and the Holy Spirit, all we know about heaven, hell and the hereafter, are in the Holy Bible. It is through Holy Writ that we come to a knowledge that we are sinners, that there is a Saviour for man, and how we may be saved.

After the experience of salvation by the word of life, it is also through the word that we have victorious Christian living in this world (1 Jn 5:4).

What Kenneth Copeland said on one of his audio

tapes thrills my heart. According to him, his father said, 'Ken, if I ever find out one day that the Bible is not true, I will still live by it because it works.'

The word works. It is the road map of life.

The abomination of this age is its restlessness and mad rush. But you can always remember the pressure of our generation, 'Thou wilt keep him in perfect peace, whose mind is stayed on thee: because he trusteth in thee' (Is 26:3). Please rest on his promises. Don't allow society to sweep you off your feet. Isaiah 28:16 says, 'He that believeth shall not make haste.'

Watch out for what the devil will sometimes want you to believe when God intervenes in your 'storm'.

'This might have happened anyway,' Satan will whisper. 'This is a remarkable coincidence, and would have happened even if you had not prayed and believed God for it.'

This is a deathtrap! Stand firm in faith, ready to give God the praise, and to confirm to others by testimony that it was a direct answer to prayer.

5

The Kingdom Key

'Blessed be the God and Father of our Lord Jesus Christ who hath blessed us with all spiritual blessings in heavenly places in Christ' (Eph 1:3).

'If we live in the Spirit, let us also walk in the Spirit' (Gal 5:25).

I am sure you have before now inferred from the Scriptures that man is a spirit. He has a soul that lives inside a body.

God is a spirit and Satan is a spirit. You realise therefore that man is surrounded by a realm of spiritual authority beyond carnal understanding. The Bible makes us understand that most trials, temptations and human crises have spiritual implications, both by occurrence and effect.

The life and ministry of our Lord Jesus Christ clearly amplify the point. The Scriptures show in Luke 4:1 that Jesus Christ faced probably the biggest test in his ministry, apart from Calvary, 'being full of the Holy Ghost . . . and was led by the Spirit'. This big test was the temptation by the devil in the wilderness — a straightforward spiritual battle!

Apostle Paul's statement in 1 Corinthians 2:8 gives strong credence to the observation that human temptations and storms of life are more than meet the eyes. He said, 'Which none of the princes of this world [forces of darkness] knew: for had they known it, they would not have crucified the Lord of glory.'

What Paul was saying in this verse is that there was spiritual interest in the crucifixion of Jesus Christ at Calvary. That is profoundly true, and the same can be said of the Christian believer.

The moment you come to know that the storms of life have spiritual undertones, it helps you to approach them from a basic spiritual front rather than by carnal instruments.

Paul's charge to the Galatians in 5:25 deals with us on every side. He expressed that the Christian should live in the Spirit as well as walk in the Spirit. We have already seen that we are spiritual beings, and so problems arise when we try to use instruments outside those provided by God's word to deal with our needs.

The new lease

When I received Jesus' command to take his healing power to my generation, I did not have any predecessor to ask questions.

I could remember occasions when I had to consult the late Revd S. Elton, a British missionary of no mean repute. In time, he became one of my early spiritual mentors, but do you know that in the affairs of life, a couple of issues crop up which no human being can help you find answers to? What I mean is, there will be times you have to sort it out with God on your own.

The early seventies was a crucial period in my ministry. I was trying to set a pace. I was trying to make headway and trying to establish exactly what I was going to do for the Lord. It was scary sometimes, but glory be to God, faith will always win over negative circumstances.

Everything seemed normal, no problem, then occasionally, I would run into storms and struggles when I began holding large-scale healing services. My mind goes back to 1972 when I decided to launch out on a massive scale. We set out with arrangements for hiring the Ogbe Stadium in Benin City for the healing service. Everywhere I went, the remarks were the same: 'Benson Idahosa, your ambition will destroy you. Take it easy. Other ministers were here before you came.'

Friend, if you will listen to the voice of discouragement, I can bet you will be like everybody else.

Even if the public thought me too ambitious, I figured I could count on the clergy and ecclesiastical support. I was in for some surprises.

The bishop of a mainline orthodox denomination I visited to solicit ministerial support said to me, 'Revd Idahosa, I sympathise with you so much. You are a young man who is unduly risking his life in the ministry.'

In what appeared to be an expression of deep concern, he drew me to his side and continued, 'My son, no one has succeeded in holding a big healing crusade in Benin City. No one will attend and besides, the witches are too strong.'

When he let go of my hand I said, 'Bishop, I choose to believe the word of God. It was the key to the success of the Apostles and is still the key to the ministry today.'

'Oh, I nearly forgot an important point,' he shouted. 'Do you know when the Apostles died, it marked the end of miracles in the Bible?'

I was stunned by such massive ignorance of God's word in higher places.

Just when I bade him goodbye, the Holy Spirit spoke to my heart words which locally answered the bishop's erroneous point of view.

The Spirit of God said to my heart, 'A problem calls for a solution. Logically and naturally as long as the problem exists, the solution will match it.'

The Holy Spirit concluded, 'Sickness did not depart from the earth after the Apostle era. How then can one say that the divine healing to check it faded away with the Apostles?'

I learned my lesson the hard way. I decided to keep my distance from those who refused to accept the Bible in its entirety.

The stupendous success of the 1972 Ogbe Stadium Crusade stopped the voices of unbelievers and accusers. When the chips were down, everyone agreed: never had there been anything like it. Over ten thousand attended with miracle healings of every kind happening daily.

When you hit a storm, whom do you believe? God or man? I choose to stand by God's word even when I do not understand or cannot figure it out.

You may be misunderstood, and some may misrepresent your motives. They may ask, 'Why are you trying to be different from the rest of us?' Stay true to God's word; don't answer back.

The media

One day I was reading the Gospel of Luke when I came to chapter 19, verse 3 which said, 'And he sought to see Jesus who he was; and could not for the press, because he was little of stature.' You can figure out who the account is about — Zaccheus — but that is not the point I want to make.

I remember reading this verse to my congregation in Benin City and showing them how 'the press' stopped Zaccheus from seeing Jesus through the crowd. This may not be exactly what the verse is saying, but it does draw attention to my observation about the press and my ministry!

Over the last two decades, I have witnessed an accelerated press attack on my ministry of the Church of God Mission International. Seldom has an objective article been written about our crusades and church activities.

I have suffered years of mud-slinging against me personally, when my only offence was that I would not compromise the word of God. Often I developed an aversion for press interviews of any kind because of the systematic perversion of truth. On occasions we have had to buy advertising space in Nigeria national newspapers to tell our side of the story because they would not quote us in their news reports.

You will discover that if you obey God, neither the press nor anything else is big enough to destroy you. The attitude of the press changed towards me as they found out that I was not going to let go of my belief and faith in Christ. Will you stand your ground on what you believe, or will you let the scaring tactics of the devil put you under?

Obedience in the face of fear

It is true that you will never live without some kind of fear. The danger is to allow it to becloud your faith, rule your heart, or affect God's voice in the vision you have received.

I have had my fair share of fearful moments, but I always remember, 'God hath not given us the spirit of fear; but of power, and of love, and of a sound mind.'

In the affairs of your daily life, moments of uncertainty will arise. You will wonder whether the voice you heard was God's or a figment of your imagination. God has spoken to me at every tough stage of the ministry. My greatest confidence as a servant of God is the unmovable acknowledgement in my heart that I hear from God. It is a cardinal key for irreversible triumph over every circumstance in life.

God has given me, at times, difficult projects to carry out or steps to follow. I would tell what God has said and people would look at me like I had gone mad or something.

Constantly, I would pour out my heart to Margaret. She would calmly say, 'Are you sure God spoke to you?'

'Absolutely sure, without an iota of doubt.'

'Then be sure to *obey God*. Play your part and he will unfailingly do the rest.'

My deacons, elders, and pastors would say encouragingly, 'Archbishop, we are with you in it all.'

When I asked for clarification, they would reply, 'Your works are your evidence. Every time you've said God spoke to you to do something, it has happened. Your track record is convincing.'

When I left the Assemblies of God on October 24, 1968, in obedience to God's instruction, how could I figure a little prayer group would become the nucleus of a world-wide rallying point for believers?

The foundation that I laid by faith at Iyaro, our second port of call, was too big for the comfort of many members of my congregation, but it became a reality!

On November 9, 1975, the famous seven-thousand-seat Miracle Centre was opened as a place for teaching, preaching, and healing.

Faith is progressive. It does not pretend that obstacles don't exist. Faith sees the obstacle or crisis and supersedes it.

If any project or assignment has given me sleepless nights and drastically tested my faith, it has been the building of the Faith Miracle Centre. Everyone thought the twenty-thousand-seat auditorium was inconceivably too far-reaching for my faith.

'Where in the world are you going to raise all the missions of Naira for this grand project?' most people queried. In the face of all adversities, God's faithfulness will always stand if you will believe his word.

One morning, just as the Faith Miracle Centre project was halfway through, my wife and I drove past the auditorium on our way to the office. As we sped past, I fixed my gaze in the opposite direction, lost in my thoughts. Margaret seemed immediately to have captured what was on my mind and said with loud laughter, 'Why did you turn your face from the auditorium when we drove past it?'

I stared at her face and said, 'I know you can understand what a test of faith this project is on my heart. When I take my eyes away from it, I am running away from the reality of life. It simply means a Greater Eye is watching over it.'

Margaret, with a note of encouragement in her voice, whispered to me, 'My dear, your shoulders will not ache. God will do his work and complete it in due season.'

True freedom

Have you ever come to a stage of your life when you feel caged in? Or maybe hemmed in by unexpected circumstances? Have you come to a point when you suddenly realise freedom is lost? Or your mind cannot get hold of the answer? We may call it a dead end.

Have you ever been confronted with a stark awareness of some spiritual bondage? Have you ever felt weighed down?

My friend, don't bemoan your life; you are not alone. I have come to one or some of all of these at one time or another in my life. They've not confronted me as a heathen, but as a spiritual man of God, and I can guarantee you, they've come in the form of church crises, marriage problems, financial needs, depression, or what appears like a thousand-and-one other maladies.

As long as you are on this earth, remember this day that you will never outgrow problems, crises and negative circumstances. If you think my statement too harsh, ponder on what God meant by, 'Many are the afflictions of the righteous, but the Lord delivereth them from all.' God will not just deliver you from some; the word says, God is faithful to deliver you from all. What this means to me is that every problem has a solution, or in other words, every prison door that slams in your face has a key from God.

It is understandable that certain awkward developments may hinder you for a little while, but for a heart set on determination and faith, we can agree, there's no situation that can permanently rob you of victory in Christ.

There is one word I have refused to use ever since I became a full-fledged Christian decades ago. It is *hopeless*! To say a situation is hopeless is to close all doors of God's intervention. Hopelessness is a human limitation and assumption.

My beloved, I can assure you on the authority of God's word that he has a way out for you through every storm of life. The key to true freedom is his word.

Earlier I mentioned briefly that one secret to staying on top of your storms and adversities, I believe, is 'to be of good cheer'. You may be thinking it is asking too much of you 'to be of good cheer' when you are on the brink of disaster, standing on the edge of certain defeat or absolute danger.

Beloved, 'be of good cheer' is a spiritual antidote to

friction and turmoil. If it were not so, how would you explain apostle Paul's letter from prison to his cherished Philippian Church: 'Rejoice in the Lord alway: and again I say, Rejoice' (Phil 4:4).

Under normal circumstances, it is the most absurd recommendation anyone can make in the position Paul was involved in. But then I charge you to let your heart be opened to the fact that 'The weapons of our warfare are not carnal, but mighty through God to the pulling down of strongholds' (2 Cor 10:4).

A great man of God once said happiness depends on happenings. This is activated by carnal pleasures like a sudden fortune, dance, or anything which satisfies the flesh. But we as Christians believe that we live by the spirit and not the flesh (Gal 5:16,25).

Therefore we discover that whereas happiness depends on happenings, joy which is fruit of the Spirit (Gal 5:22) is a spiritual word which looks up to the 'Lord alway' (Phil 4:4).

Apostle Paul was not a new convert when he made that precious statement in Philippians 4:4. He had walked with God long enough to know that he had his finger on the button. He knew beyond any doubt that God had stated in Nehemiah 8:10, ' . . . neither be ye sorry; for the joy of the Lord is your strength.'

Does Nehemiah's word strike some new revelation in your heart? I pray it will!

Many Christians quote only the latter part of the verse. But the preceding part is vital to our general understanding of the framework within which the statement was made. You know, self-pity has destroyed millions of once-hopeful Christians. Get a new revelation from the fact self-pity will get you nowhere, except down the drain of defeat and drowsiness.

Nehemiah said, 'Neither be ye sorry.' It is a personal decision. Please don't be sorry. Rather do what? Put on God's joy, which will give you strength in the face of the odds.

Are you willing and ready to follow God's perspective and his mind on your situation? This takes more than nodding your head or mentally assenting, or operating by mass mind. You may come to a certain point in life when truly you don't know what to do. Can you say the same of God? No!

'But I agree with all that you have been sharing with me. How do I get answers from someone I can't see?' This may be your frank question.

I am confident to tell you that God's word has all the answers to any crisis, problem, or need of life. It will work for you in China, or Alaska, or among the pygmies in Central Africa. God's word transcends all geographical and human barriers. It is a spiritual law in effect. It cannot change, but it changes everything it comes into contact with if acted on by faith.

Matthew 16:19 says, 'And I will give unto thee the keys of the kingdom of heaven: and whatsoever thou shalt bind on earth shall be bound in heaven: and whatsoever thou shalt loose on earth shall be loosed in heaven.'

Keys are important instruments. The general manager may have the keys to the bank, but it is the cashier who has the key to the office door.

Jesus Christ knew what he was talking about when

he spoke about keys of the kingdom of heaven. Jesus did not say 'key'. He said 'keys'.

Rest assured that God's word is full of keys of kingdom principles — keys to destroy satanic operation and loose your blessings.

I remember Dr Kenneth Copeland saying, 'When you find the kingdom key, you have found a soft spot in the devil's armour.' This is the truth!

Many times the devil will tell me there is no way out. He will sidetrack me. He will manoeuvre to get my eyes off God's word. The devil will tell you all that has come over you is God's word. Please don't believe the devil! 'For all the promises of God in him are yea, and in him Amen, unto the glory of God by us' (2 Cor 1:20).

6

Outliving Your Storm

'Brethren, I count not myself to have apprehended: but this one thing I do, forgetting those things which are behind, and reaching forth unto those things which are before, I press toward the mark for the prize of the high calling of God in Christ Jesus' (Phil 3:13–14).

The verses quoted above are part and parcel of Paul's letter to the Philippian Church. Paul had deep love for this church which was torn out of his back-breaking Macedonian trip (as recounted in Acts 16).

You appreciate that Paul was not writing to non-Christians, but to a virile church of born-again Bible-believing people. In Philippians 3:13 he addressed them as brethren, which indicates a bond of fellowship. The great Apostle's admonition to the Philippian Church will serve the same purpose in your ministry and life. He encouraged them to look beyond the travails and trials which accompany the Christian experience.

You may say, 'The storms of life or crises are for new converts.' My friend, that is far from the truth.

Others will simply shout, 'Trials are for mature Christians.' You are the first to admit that both positions are erroneous. The moment you become born again, you come into a collision path with the devil and his cohorts.

But the apostle Paul expressed that we should not allow these adversities to hinder our growth or stop us in our tracks. He was bold to advise that we forget the hindrances of yesterday and reach forth for a new tomorrow of hope and aspirations.

If you assume regrettably that Paul did not have the credentials and authority to counsel you, read 2 Corinthians 11:23–27:

> . . . I am more: in labours more abundant, in stripes above measure, in prisons more frequent, in deaths oft.
>
> Of the Jews five times received I forty stripes save one.
>
> Thrice was I beaten with rods, once was I stoned, thrice I suffered shipwreck, a night and a day I have been in the deep;
>
> In journeys often, in perils of waters, in perils of robbers, in perils of mine own countrymen, in perils by the heathen, in perils in the city, in perils in the wilderness, in perils in the sea, in perils among false brethren;
>
> In weariness and painfulness, in watchings often, in hunger and thirst, in fastings often, in cold and nakedness.

These are the words of experience of one of the greatest servants of God who ever walked this earth. To Paul, trials are for testimonies. If you thought Paul was going to warn you to go underground, fizzle out, or backslide because of the storms of life, you are in for a surprise.

How many preachers or Christians can stand what Paul stood in his day? Don't get me wrong. I admit you could face maybe the same number of trials under different circumstances. Yes, I subscribe to that.

The point I am aiming at is your response. To Paul, his uncompromising stand is to strenuously press forward in the face of mounting opposition on every side.

Do you acknowledge, however, that many tests that come our way are not our fault? The Apostles had good reason to say that we enter into the kingdom by much tribulation. There are occasions when inexplicable hardship comes up and it takes God's abounding grace to overcome. But in the spirit and frame of mind that Paul said it, hardships and trials are sometimes preparation of life for later experiences. All you need to do is depend upon God and rejoice in the flow of the Holy Spirit through each day. The difficulty and confusion arise when you opt to defend yourself or fight your way out. Calmly count on his divine grace. Calmly count on his presence. Calmly look to the God of your salvation.

Paul wrote in 1 Corinthians 16:13, 'Watch ye, stand fast in the faith, quit you like men, be strong.' I am advocating you thank God for putting you in the fix. I mean, thank him for the way out of it all, by his Spirit and his grace.

Persecution

It is obvious from Paul's statement in 1 Corinthians 12:10, 'I take pleasure in persecutions,' that they are

God's will. That is not to say you deliberately generate persecution. You don't have to. In fact, the Bible declares that all who live godly lives will be persecuted. What you must understand is that when God speaks of suffering as Paul enumerated in 2 Corinthians 11, it does not have to do with sickness.

It is not my intention to glorify afflictions or persecutions. But you must agree painfully, that when we live right, it runs against the system of the world. What the apostle Peter said in 1 Peter 4:14 will shed light on my observation. He said, 'If ye be reproached for the name of Christ, happy are ye; for the spirit of glory and of God resteth upon you.'

The primary purpose of this book is to prepare you for the unavoidable trials and upheavals which come with the whole of life. It is to build you up with a consciousness to see beyond the immediate crisis into the testimony of victory when it is all over.

Fellowship or followship

It grieves my heart to know that some Christians don't understand this. Just look around you, maybe at your own life. Generally, you appreciate the joy and presence of the Lord when the going is smooth. Then, *bang!* the tide changes. You run into unexpected problems and you seem to be unprepared for them. We will say, it is a nose dive from the mountain into the valley pitch. Suddenly, you feel stuck.

Honestly, if you want to know, it is in the valley we know those who are genuinely walking in the faith of Christ.

In John, Chapter 6, we read of a small crisis which Jesus had with his disciples. This singular problem was to fashion out the disciples from fellowship to a higher position of fellowship. There was a great fallout with many withdrawing from fellowship (Jn 6:66). Crises may be designed by the enemy to destroy you, but God has a noble purpose throughout the heat of it all.

'Then said Jesus unto the twelve, Will ye also go away?' (Jn 6:67). This was the straightforward question Jesus put to the disciples who remained steadfast.

Today I dare ask you, 'Will you also go away from Jesus Christ and the Christian walk because of some hitch on your way?' You don't have to if the words of Peter mean anything to you: '. . . Lord, to whom shall we go? Thou hast the words of eternal life' (Jn 6:68).

Peter may have been impetuous, but you will be glad to know he made statements which made much more sense and showed deep spiritual awareness.

Going back is not the answer. The Christian is made to go forward, regardless of what confronts him. Peter said solemnly, 'To whom shall we go?'

That same question is coming to you today. Hold on in faith, grow from fellowship to the strong foundation of followership. When the feast of surplus bread from feeding five thousand is over, there will be some moments of realistic appraisal. Make up your mind to stand by him who has the words of eternal life.

Victories behind

There are times I wonder whether the battles of life will ever cease.

Beloved, I can assure you of a day when we will cease from our labour, but that is after this life's journey is over. Here and now is the battle! Now is the hour of struggles on every side, but if you believe God's word, the victory is guaranteed.

The Bible says to 'fight the good fight!' Of what? Of faith! Unbelief has no part in the faith fight. The devil will whip you clean if you face any crisis of life on any ground beside God's word.

Unbelief by simple definition is believing anything no matter what we think to the contrary.

If I believe in God and his word concerning a particular situation, whereas someone else believes in the custom or tradition of his forefathers regarding the situation, the other person is walking in unbelief in relation to the same situation.

Traditions and customs may change or be outmoded, but for ever the word of God is settled in heaven. Maybe in your heart you are pondering, 'Ah, in our family this is how we deal with this issue from a traditional point of view.'

Are you a Christian believer? If you are, then your statement exemplifies your unbelief. If you are a believing Christian with faith in God's word, you will act as if you believe God's word!

The battle we have with Satan is a fight to the finish. In recent times, when the Church of God Mission International was faced with a crisis, I told the thousands of members on a Sunday morning, 'We are warriors. We don't retreat. We advance because God did not raise me to train fleeing soldiers.'

Glory be to God, we never lose if we depend upon

the power of God to help us. The Bible makes it abundantly clear that the power that is in us is greater than the power that is in the world (1 Jn 4:4). If we allow the power of God to flow through our lives, we will have victory. Sure victory!

Road to Macedonia

Acts 16:9,10 says:

> And a vision appeared to Paul in the night; There stood a man of Macedonia, and prayed him, saying, Come over into Macedonia, and help us.
>
> And after he had seen the vision, immediately we endeavoured to go into Macedonia, assuredly gathering that the Lord had called us for to preach the gospel unto them.

This is one of the most eye-opening incidents in the Bible about those occasions when we can expect in our effort to fulfil God's will, in any area of life.

Paul had a vision inviting him to Macedonia to preach. Who gives the vision to take the world for Jesus Christ? Of course, the vision was from God, and Paul believed the finger of the Lord was in it.

It is not a bed of roses when it comes to doing the will of God. Sometimes so much satanic attack is launched against you, you think the whole of hell has hemmed you in. This was exactly what Paul faced.

> And it came to pass, as we went to prayer, a certain damsel possessed with a spirit of divination met us, which brought her masters much gain by soothsaying:
>
> The same followed Paul and us, and cried, saying, These

men are the servants of the most high God. which shew
unto us the way of salvation.

And this did she many days. But Paul, being grieved,
turned and said to the spirit, I command thee in the
name of Jesus Christ to come out of her. And he came
out the same hour (Acts 16:16–18).

Paul was a man who had great zeal in the things of
God. From the account in Acts 16, he proceeded to
the chief city of Macedonia called Philippi. Paul whistled
along the streets of Philippi, his heart pounding with
joy and excitement about the new door of opportunity
which was opening before them. Maybe it was a dream
come true. An answered prayer for a heart cry to take
Macedonia for Jesus Christ.

In verse 16, Paul and his team run into their maiden
hurdle, a girl with a spirit of divination. Satan has a
way of confusing matters for those who are not deep
in spiritual matters.

The Bible explains how this possessed girl became
a self-appointed usher and introducer of the Pauline
team.

Many years ago when I read this strange verse I
wondered why the devil would introduce a ministry of
Jesus. It was not for the fun of it. It was on purpose,
because Satan does not do anything like that unless
he knows it is to his advantage.

The possessed girl said, 'These men are the servants
of the most high God, which shew unto us the way of
salvation' (Acts 16:17). Now the relevant question is not
whether the girl's statement was true or not. It was
true, beyond all doubt that Paul, Silas, and others were
servants of God who led men to salvation.

What then was the devil's vested interest if the girl's statement was true and an obvious advantage in publicity for Paul and the team?

The Bible says we are not ignorant of the devices of the devil. The main aim of the satanic ploy is to give credibility to the activities of the demon-possessed girl by her association with the servants of God. The devilish agent gains some respectability, whereas the servants of God will have their goal impeded when the truth comes out ultimately.

It is like saying, 'Oh, folks, see what I'm doing is exactly what Paul and company have come to do. We are all the same.' This was what the girl was driving at. Here we see the truth in the Scripture that Satan has turned himself into an angel of light.

The Bible says it was several days before Paul cast out the spirit of divination from the girl. Maybe Paul did not initially discern what spirit was operating in the girl. But the Spirit of God opened Paul's eyes, which resulted in the spirit being cast out.

The divergent tactics of Satan were at work at this point. Paul had his eyes on Macedonia. In the vision he saw a man beckoning him to Macedonia and not a demon-possessed girl. Does that mean Paul was mistaken? No, he wasn't, but that was the impression the devil wanted to give him.

To you reading this book, I say, 'Keep your eye on the vision, don't be snared by trivial distractions.'

From the general perspective, Paul's worst moment was yet to come. The deliverance of the girl led Paul and others into fury upon the servants of God.

And when they had laid many stripes upon them, they cast them into prison, charging the jailer to keep them safely . . .

And at midnight Paul and Silas prayed, and sang praises unto God: and the prisoners heard them (Acts 16:23,25).

If you want to think about a storm of life, I can say this is it. The apostle Paul and his team had probably testified in the church prior to their departure, the glorious vision of open doors in Macedonia.

But now, here they are sitting somewhere in a dark alley of a stinking prison dungeon with stocks bracing their hands and feet.

At this point the devil will whisper as usual, 'Paul, are you sure God is calling you to go to Macedonia? And if so, why has he abandoned you in this rancid dungeon?'

Thank God for Paul and the great example he left for all the Christians in similar tight spots. Paul and company did not go on a pity party, bemoaning their fate and pleading for sympathy. They did what many Christians will not dream of even as a last resort. They prayed and sang praises to God in that state of shame.

The devil was not ready for the option Paul and his colleagues chose. It was a spiritual alternative. They beat Satan hands down. The devil could not believe his eyes when he saw blood-drenched hands and backs.

This is the army that will not draw back. God's will was a command without detours.

You need singleness of purpose and a heart fixed on complete obedience even in adverse circumstances.

Where is the man who beckoned to Paul in the vision

to come over to Macedonia and help? You are in for a surprise at the outworking of God's purposes.

The Bible informs us that heaven responded to the anointed praises of his people. Heaven swiftly moved into action on behalf of the men of God. The lesson here is that if you respond properly in the hour of crisis, deliverance is likely to come more quickly. A scriptural and spiritual response to crisis does not hamper divine intervention, as Paul and company proved.

A large-scale earthquake shook the prison, rendering the doors and the stocks binding prisoners loose. Beloved, be encouraged to know this day that God will never leave you nor forsake you. He has said in Psalm 50:15, 'And call upon me in the day of trouble: I will deliver thee, and thou shalt glorify me.' The reality of this Davidic psalm is in clear demonstration here in the Philippian jailhouse. The power of God transcends political and geographical barriers.

The central text in the whole drama is what we read in Acts 16:27–32:

> And the keeper of the prison awakening out of his sleep, and seeing the prison doors open, he drew out his sword, and would have killed himself, supposing that the prisoners had fled.
>
> But Paul cried with a loud voice, saying, Do thyself no harm: for we are all here.
>
> Then he called for a light, and sprang in, and came trembling, and fell down before Paul and Silas,
>
> And brought them out, and said, Sirs, what must I do to be saved?
>
> And they said, Believe on the Lord Jesus Christ, and thou shalt be saved, and thy house.

And they spake unto him the word of the Lord, and to all that were in his house.

Earthquake settles the issue

God has a way out for you in every hitch on your way, if you follow his directions. A golden opportunity came for the apostle Paul and Silas to abscond as the earthquake unleashed the prison doors and the chains on their hands and feet.

I can say the devil will once again whisper, 'Boys, this is an opportunity for you to run to freedom.'

Glory be to God! Paul and Silas did not want an easy way out of it all because they were convinced God was in it all with them.

Even if his purpose was not visibly clear to their understanding they knew the Higher mind would work it out for certain.

Secondly, if they had fled, far-reaching implications would have resulted. They would have been declared fugitives and immediately aborted the Macedonia mission. By the natural reaction of running away from jail they would have gone back to their home base, rather than in the direction of divine command.

God's purposes are indeed mysterious, to say the least. When the Philippian jailer heard the singing and praising he might have thought of it as the excitement of some overzealous company. However, the earthquake caught his attention. The jailer recognised that Paul and Silas had heavenly backing. Their refusal to flee was the last pillar of unbelief in the jailer's heart.

He said, 'Sirs, what must I do to be saved?' Notice

the prison boss was calling prisoners 'Sirs'. Beloved, I tell you God can honour you even in prison. They honoured God with praises and the Lord reciprocated. Obey God and your jailer will call you 'Sir'.

Now for the surprise! Do you know the man of Macedonia that Paul saw in the vision was the Philippian jailer? Yes, he is the man who beckoned to the servants of God to come and help.

Paul and Silas did not find him as a police road conductor or a king in the area. The jailer was not a famous athlete who was a household name. The servants of God went by faith, overcame the crisis by faith in the God who sent them, and succeeded through overwhelming faith in Christ.

This episode of Paul's ministry should bring you some sublime lessons of life.

God is supremely bigger than every crisis you meet.

God will walk with you every step through it.

God will give you grace in every storm of life.

Beloved, be encouraged because 'tribulation worketh patience' (Rom 5:3).

Recognise it is he 'which worketh in you both to will and to do of his good pleasure' (Phil 2:13).

I think I sincerely agree with the Revd Ralph Mahoney, who postulated that, 'Affliction separates the chosen from the called. "I have chosen thee in the furnace of affliction" (Is 48:10).' Mr Mahoney says in this verse, the word 'chosen' is used in the sense of being 'graded', as in a school examination or test.

You can certainly outlive your storms. Don't brood and cry over them. God takes you forward into new horizons. Meditate on James 1:2–4:

My brethren, count it all joy when ye fall into divers
temptations;

Knowing this, that the trying of your faith worketh
patience.

But let patience have her perfect work, that ye may be
perfect and entire, wanting nothing.

Learn to develop perseverance and grow out of every
crisis. The more I find myself in a state of trials and
tribulations, the more I realise that my calling is like
that of the three Hebrew children and that of Daniel,
Elijah, Elisha, David, Moses, Peter, Paul, and that of
Jesus Christ our Lord and Saviour who wore thorns
before he wore the crown of glory in his Father's right
hand in heavenly places.

Trials do not kill the man or woman called by God.
Rather, they strengthen him or her. And the saints
can make a big example of God's power.

7

Having Done All, Stand

Your faith must be based on the word of God if it is
going to be a steady faith, a consistent faith not subject
to undue wavering but solid in both good and bad
times. This is a basic truth I have repeatedly stressed
through the pages of this book.

There is such a thing as an enduring faith. That kind
of faith depends steadfastly upon the word of God.

Faith is progressive, and living faith is active, defying
all human hindrances. The word of God works in the
same way with your faith.

Needless to say, I believe in all the principles in this
book. They have worked unfailingly in my life. I take
time to preach the word of God to myself. The Bible
indeed says, 'Faith cometh by hearing, and hearing by
the word of God' (Rom 10:17).

Faith comes by hearing the word of God. From
whom? The evangelist or pastor or any instrument of
God. You can speak the word of faith to your spirit,
too. If you can believe anybody, it should be yourself.

Read the promises of God and build yourself up on your most holy faith. The preaching of the word by men and women who are anointed causes faith to soar up in your heart.

Often the devil has said to me, 'Hey, Benson Idahosa, you are trying to act like God. You are using God's word.'

I reply boldly, 'Yes, that is what I am doing. I am using God's word to resist you and triumph over my circumstances.'

The worried mind is not the mind of Christ because the Scripture says, 'Let this mind be in you, which was also in Christ Jesus' (Phil 2:5).

To stand when everything crumbles around you is not an easy passage. 'A thousand shall fall at thy side, and ten thousand at thy right hand; but it shall not come nigh thee' (Ps 91:7), takes something more than going to church or singing in a great choir.

It takes a firm knowing in your spirit what God has said about you—particularly concerning the finished work of Jesus Christ at Calvary and his resurrection.

The truth is that nobody knows more than Satan himself what was accomplished in the death, burial and resurrection of Christ.

Even though Satan knows, he will not have you know it, because knowledge is power. The Bible states in John 8:32, 'And ye shall know the truth, and the truth shall make you free.'

God is saying in this verse that truth is freedom. And may I kindly add that your freedom in the full spectrum of life depends upon the amount of truth you know from the Bible.

Satan struggles relentlessly to keep you from learning about all that God has promised you in Christ Jesus. He will put sickness on you and say God is using it to teach you a lesson. He will deprive you of God's prosperity if you allow him to and then whisper to you that God made you poor to humble you.

Let me put it this way: as long as Satan can make you doubt what Christ has done for you in the supreme sacrifice of his life for you, he can conveniently beat you in every battle. What I mean is, he puts you in a state of non-resistance. God has said in James 4:7, 'Resist the devil, and he will flee from you.'

In some thirty years of walking with Christ, I have come across Christians everywhere who belong to the 'It is always God's will' group. They never take the trouble to find out what God has said concerning them in the Bible. They pick a few Scriptures along the way. Maybe the pastor used a notable verse in his sermon, and so they seize that one. A sister in the church uses another scripture and they add it to their scanty storehouse of God's word. It is not, therefore, surprising that the devil is able to convince these churchgoers that everything from sickness, poverty, defeat, broken homes and sin is all God's will

Find what God's will is from the Bible and vow in your heart to stand upon it resolutely. We are to be strong in the Lord and in the power of his might. It didn't say be strong in the world and in the power of political authority.

Put on the whole armour of God. It is the only overcoming equipment against the wiles of the devil.

My special statement

Have you been faced with power from the enemy's camp and you shout as if God has forsaken you? Have you seen Satan face to face like Jesus did in Matthew 4:1 and Luke 4? Have you come to a place where you almost gave in and gave up to the enemy's expectation in your walk and work for God?

Have you been forced to say to Jesus, 'If it be thy will, bid one come to you in storm.' I have come very close to the point where I almost gave up when unexpected storms came into my life. Yet, I have come to know that there are a few of us with a special calling from God and that we cannot run away. But run nearer, my God, to thee. I encourage you to rise to your feet and start your walk of faith to victory. Start today. Victory is very close to you.

When we accept the risen Lord into our lives as Saviour and Lord, he dwells in us. That instantly puts his whole armour upon us and *Christ is our victory*. God is telling you now, 'Behold, I am the Lord, the God of all flesh, is there anything too hard for me?' Read Isaiah 54:17. It says protection is your heritage.

God has not given you the spirit of fear.

You have the mind of Christ, a victorious mind.

You have put off the sin nature and put on the divine nature.

Christ is your strength at all times.

What a glorious inheritance!

Revolutionise your revelation of Christ in your life.

A new tomorrow

You might have had rough yesterdays, yesteryears. From birth maybe all your plans have become stillborn. Then it is for you especially that this book is written. The miracle of God is like a river passing by your door daily with grace, blessing, signs and wonders.

Wherever I go, I say boldly, 'I cannot live one day without miracles.'

This chapter has prophetic implication in your life. By the authority of God's word, I say to you, 'There will be no more lost battles in your life.'

The devil may bark and roar, but remember the words of the apostle John: 'When you are born of God in new birth, that wicked one touches you not' (1 Jn 5:18).

Stand on the word that your life is hid with Christ in God. Now Satan knows as he approaches you, he has Jesus to deal with. You are a winner in Christ.

Take hold of God's word in 1 Corinthians 15:57: 'Thanks be to God, which giveth us the victory through our Lord Jesus Christ.'

You can triumph over the adversities of life. That is all I have been trying to imprint upon your heart.

When the devil comes to you, he must deal with Christ who conquered him. You don't have to walk alone. When Satan touches you, he knows he is touching God's property.

Let me illustrate our new position of victory by this revelation God gave me recently. In my neighbourhood, which is commonly called the Government Residential Area (GRA), there are some buildings occupied by serving military officers.

At the gates of these top level military officers, you will find this conspicuous inscription in bold red letters, 'Military zone. Keep off.'

I have grown up with this common inscription and it did not mean anything to me until recently when I was preaching on 'spiritual warfare'.

Driving past one of the gates, my eyes caught sight of the inscription again. Immediately, a revelation popped up in my heart.

The Spirit of God said to me, 'My servant Idahosa, if the soldiers ask intruders to keep off because it is a military zone, what do you say of yourself? You are not a worldly soldier.'

I could not make out what God was saying. The question resurfaced in my spirit after a while. After a few minutes I shouted, 'For the Christian, it is *Spiritual zone. Keep off.*' I felt the Spirit of God confirm this to me.

Meditating on the fact that we are spiritual zones (to warn all satanic invasion) brought no small peace to my heart.

God has made you a spiritual zone if you are born again. God has put an inscription on your forehead: *Spiritual zone. Keep off.*

The circumstances around you will respond to God's word building up in your heart. The seed of God's word will bear basket-breaking fruit in your affairs.

Jesus Christ said in Luke 6:46–49,

And why call ye me, Lord, Lord, and do not the things which I say?

Whosoever cometh to me, and heareth my sayings, and doeth them, I will shew you to whom he is like:

He is like a man which built an house, and digged deep, and laid the foundation on a rock: and when the flood arose, the stream beat vehemently upon that house, and could not shake it: for it was founded upon a rock.

But he that heareth, and doeth not, is like a man that without a foundation built an house upon the earth; against which the stream did beat vehemently, and immediately it fell; and the ruin of that house was great.

There is a vital lesson hidden in this great parable by Jesus Christ. Some will think the key issue was the storm. No, it wasn't. It was the foundation on which the two houses were built.

Your life, like the two houses in the parable, is built on some foundation. What is it?

Other people would focus attention on trivialities like storm windows, new roofings, and the like in the parable. These were purely side issues.

You must admit that the key issue was the foundation of the building.

A solid foundation is a homeowner's greatest guarantee in the face of storm and hurricane.

In this closing chapter, remember obedience to the word of God is a solid foundation.

Beloved, if you diligently do what Jesus said, the principles outlined in this book will work in your life. Do the sayings of Jesus and you will have a house with a firm foundation. The floods and storms of life do not come from God.

Plant God's word in your heart every day and do the sayings of Jesus Christ, and you will not fail!

You must vow to do God's word yourself. This is your part of the agreement. Start believing that every promise to the believer you read in the Bible will come to pass in your life.

With a heart of expectation I dedicate this poem God gave me recently to you:

Tomorrow

Tomorrow, the day without an ugly story.
Tomorrow, the dreams of yesterday will
find fulfilment.
Tomorrow, the Hand of the Almighty will
take me there.
Tomorrow, a day of greater hope.
Tomorrow, designed for new horizons.
Have faith in tomorrow.
If you don't have a plan with God today,
Tomorrow, my friend, is but
a passing dream!

The day you come to the conclusion that God is stronger than the devil and that God is in you as the Mightier One, the Stronger, the Wiser, the All-knowing God, the Creator, the Possessor of the heaven and the earth, is the day that your song will change, your tears will stop, your fear will flee from you. And that is the day that God will say to you, 'Son/daughter, you and I are an unbeatable team. I am now in you and you in me.' Therefore, you can face any storm with God-given assurance that when the battle is over, you will be on top, singing and dancing, saying, 'I am a winner 365 days of the year!' And you can start it today. Arise and shine! Let God arise and his enemy will scatter.

Finally hear these words

If Jesus did not fail those who came before you, if he
did not fail those who started before you, I am very
sure he will not fail you. He will not let you down. He
will not pick you up to knock you down. He is the
same yesterday, today and for evermore (Heb 13:8).
He is too strong to become too weak in your turn. He
is too good to be too bad. He is too close to be too far
away from you now. Look up to the God of your
salvation. Your salvation draws near. Your song will
soon start, your victory will soon be seen by even your
enemies. I can see you standing tomorrow, saying I
was bad yesterday, yet God has shown me his favour
today. May your joy never cease, may your victories be
many until you stand before Jesus saying, 'I am more
than a conqueror through Christ Jesus. Hallelujah!
Hallelujah!'